A Jewish man picked up the phone and dialed. When a voice answered, he asked, "Mother, how are you?"

"Fine."

"Sorry, I have the wrong number."

* * *

What's a Jewish porno film?

55 minutes of begging, 5 minutes of sex, and 1 hour of guilt.

* * *

What did one mink say to another as they were about to be taken off to be killed and skinned?

"See you at the Temple."

500 GREAT
JEWISH
JOKES

BY

JAY ALLEN

A SIGNET BOOK

To Teri Sutfin, a special person with
a special sense of humor

SIGNET
Published by the Penguin Group
Penguin Books USA Inc., 375 Hudson Street, New York, New
York 10014, U.S.A.
Penguin Books Ltd, 27 Wrights Lane, London W8 5TZ, England
Penguin Books Australia Ltd, Ringwood, Victoria, Australia
Penguin Books Canada Ltd, 2801 John Street, Markham, Ontario,
Canada L3R 1B4
Penguin Books (N.Z.) Ltd, 182-190 Wairau Road, Auckland 10,
New Zealand

Penguin Books Ltd, Registered Offices: Harmondsworth, Middlesex,
England

First published by Signet, an imprint of Penguin Books USA Inc.

First Printing, June, 1990
10 9 8 7 6 5 4 3 2 1

 REGISTERED TRADEMARK—MARCA REGISTRADA

Printed in the United States of America

CONTENTS

1. Great Jokes About Jewish-American Princesses   7

2. Great Jokes About Jewish Marriages   29

3. Great Jewish Jokes About Money and Business   53

4. Great Ethnic Jokes About Jews   85

5. Great Jokes About Jewish Mothers and Children   107

6. Great Jokes About Jewish Homosexuals   129

7. Great Jokes About Older Jews   139

8. Great Jokes About Israel   149

9. Great Jokes About Jews and Sex   159

CHAPTER 1

GREAT JOKES ABOUT JEWISH-AMERICAN PRINCESSES

What kind of video turns on a JAP?
A tape of the fur sales at Bloomingdale's.

What's the difference between a JAP and *Jaws*?
Nail polish.

Why is a JAP like stale beer?
You get no head from either one.

What do you get when you cross a JAP and a computer?
A system that never goes down.

What kind of drugs do JAPs snort?
Diet Coke.

What do JAPs call a handjob?
A manicure.

9

What's the first thing a JAP does after sex?
Moves.

What's the difference between a JAP and a terrorist?
A terrorist makes fewer demands.

Did you hear about the porno movie about a JAP housewife?
It's called *Debbie Does Nothing*.

Did you hear about the guy who asked a Jewish girl out to dinner and had sex that very night?
He jerked off half an hour after he dropped her off.

How does a JAP know dinner is ready?
The smoke alarm goes off.

What's the first thing a JAP learns about gardening?
To turn the soil over—to a gardener.

What's the difference between a JAP and a toilet seat?
A toilet seat warms up when you touch it.

How can you tell if a JAP bride is really ugly?
Everyone lines up to kiss the caterer.

How long does a JAP spend in finishing school?
Once she finds a man, she's finished.

How does a Jap know when it's raining?
Water gets in her nose.

A beggar walked up to a JAP as she was about to walk into Bloomingdale's and said, "Lady, I haven't eaten in six days."
She looked at him and said, "I wish I had your willpower."

What do you get when you come in a JAP?
Ice cream.

How do you rate screwing a JAP?
Below zero.

What's the difference between a JAP and a block of ice?
Eventually, ice melts.

A JAP was out to dinner with her husband. At the end of the meal the waiter approached and asked, "Was *anything* all right?"

Why does a JAP close her eyes during sex?
She pretends she's shopping.

To her family's delight, the JAP landed a prize husband, the son of an English duke. After the honeymoon, the couple came to the United States to live. The JAP began to instruct her husband, who had grown up on a huge country estate, on more informal ways of life in the USA.

On the second day back, she took her husband to a supermarket. "Darling," she said, "I'll push this cart. You walk along and put all your favorites into the cart." He trotted off ahead of her, then returned with an armful of packages.

She inspected them, pointing. "Drop this in the cart. And this. And this." Suddenly she spied a large steak. Her face formed an expression of deep disgust, and she said, "No. You must never by anything like that?"

"But why?" her husband asked.

"It needs to be cooked."

Why do JAPs believe tennis is like life?
"Love" means nothing.

Why don't JAPs exercise?
If God had wanted them to bend over, he'd have put diamonds on the floor.

What's the difference between a Jewish-American Princess and an Italian-American Princess?
With an Italian American Princess, the jewels are fake and the orgasms are real.

What do you call a JAP locked in a basement?
A whine cellar.

Young Harry Stein finally got up the nerve to propose to the boss's daughter. She said yes with a big smile on her face, but that smile turned to a glare when she opened the ring box.

"What's this little thing?" she demanded. "It couldn't be more than one carat."

"I know, darling," Harry said. "But you know what they say, love is blind."

"Not stone blind," the JAP replied.

How can you tell if you're in a JAP's kitchen? There's three taps in the sink—hot, cold and Alka-Seltzer.

Why don't they let JAPs study French or Spanish in school?
One tongue is more than enough for a JAP.

Did you hear about the JAP who tripped over the carpet and fell headfirst on the floor?
She wasn't hurt—her nose broke the fall.

Why is a JAP a scientific wonder?
She can lie in the sun on Miami Beach for nine straight hours and not thaw.

What's a JAP's recipe for chicken soup?
"Bring pot of Perrier to a full boil. . . ."

How can you tell if a bride is a JAP?
She stops halfway down the aisle to ask if
anyone has an aspirin.

What's the difference between a WASP and a
JAP?
A WASP keeps a diary; a JAP keeps a bankbook.

What are the first two words a JAP learns?
"Charge it."

What does a JAP like most about being married?
Having a maid.

What does the husband of a JAP like most
about being married?
Having the maid.

What do you get when you cross a JAP and a hooker?
A girl who goes down on credit cards.

Did you hear about the new JAP phone?
It doesn't ring, it whines.

Why is it fortunate so many JAPs are married to doctors?
The only way to get a JAP to make love is general anesthesia.

One guy ran into friend one day. To his surprise, the friend was shuffling along with his legs wide apart and moaning with every step. The guy said, "Fred, what happened to you?"

"It's my cock," Fred moaned. "I had one date with that JAP from the office and my prick turned black."

"That's awful. What is it, gonorrhea?"

"No, worse."

"Syphilis?"

"No, worse."

"What could be worse than syphilis?"

Fred winced, then replied, "Frostbite."

What's the difference between a JAP and a lesbian?
A JAP's goal is a fur coat, while a lesbian will settle for a fur piece.

What's a JAP's most horrible nightmare?
It begins when she's kidnapped from her car and taken to K-Mart. . . .

The young man got down on his knees in front of the JAP and said, "Darling, I love you. I will give you diamonds, furs, and all the money you'll ever need. What can you give me in return?"

"A receipt," the JAP replied.

What's the JAP's "rhythm method"?
Having sex only the night before she has her hair done.

How do you get a JAP to engage in oral sex?
Wrap a diamond bracelet around your cock.

What's the difference between a JAP and a light bulb?
A light bulb moves when you screw it.

Why are naval maneuvers like being the fiancé of a JAP?
Naval maneuvers are engagements with no loss of seamen.

Why did the JAP wear Voyager panties?
She thought her ass was out of this world.

"Is it in?" he asked.
"Yes," the JAP replied.
"Does it hurt?" he asked.
"No," she replied.
Then she bought the pair of shoes.

Why is a JAP like Silly Putty?
No matter how much you squeeze her, you'll never feel her crack.

A guy walked up to a JAP at a party and said, "I've got to ask you a very frank question. Do you enjoy sex?"

Her nose wrinkled as if she was smelling something unpleasant, then she said, "No, I don't."

He grabbed her arm and said, "Neither do I. So let's go to the bedroom and get it over with."

What does a JAP consider a major failure? When she has to get her fur coat from her husband the hard way.

Why are JAPs so reluctant to engage in sex? They know it's habit-forming.

Sophie ran into her friend Rachel at the temple and asked, "So, Rachel, how is it working out with that therapist I recommended."

"Wonderful," Rachel replied. "I mean, before I started seeing Dr. Moskow, I was the most self-centered, egotistical person. Now I realize I am the most terrific person I know!"

Did you hear about the JAP whose cunt talked back?
She called it her answering cervix.

How can you tell you're necking with a JAP?
When she opens her mouth, a little light goes on inside it.

What is six inches long, has a bald head, and drives a JAP crazy?
A hundred-dollar bill.

Why did her friend describe the JAP as electric?
Everything she touched, she charged.

What's the shapliest thing in a JAP's sweater?
The hanger marks.

Why don't JAPs buy brooms?
They don't come with instructions.

What's a JAP strip joint?
You pay ten dollars a drink to watch a JAP take off her jewelry.

Why is a JAP like poison ivy?
They're both something awful to have on your hands.

Why is sex with a JAP like a movie theater?
She makes you pay before you enter.

Why do JAPs have two sets of lips?
So they can piss and moan at the same time.

Did you hear about the new JAP horror movie?
It's called *Debbie Does Dishes*.

What's the closest a JAP gets to French kissing?
Eating kosher tongue.

What's a JAP's breakfast?
A Diet Coke and a Twinkie.

Why don't JAPs care that Jewish men have to undergo circumcision?
It's no skin off their nose.

Why do JAPs love vibrators?
It's sex with someone they love.

What's the difference between a pussy and a cunt?
A pussy is soft and wet and warm and wonderful —a cunt is the JAP who owns it.

How do you know you've been to bed with a JAP?
Dawn comes, and you haven't.

What's the definition of a JAP?
A woman who thinks cooking and fucking are two cities in China.

What do you call a thousand JAPs in Bloomingdale's on sale days?
Yidlock.

What's so special about the elevator at Bloomingdale's?
It's the only thing a JAP will go down on.

What's perfect sex to a JAP?
Simultaneous headaches.

How can you tell when a JAP is having an orgasm?
She uncrosses her legs.

How do you know when a JAP is having an orgasm?
She drops her nail file.

What's a JAP's idea of natural childbirth?
Absolutely no makeup.

What's a JAP's dream house?
Fourteen rooms, swimming pool, servants'
quarters, no kitchen, no bedroom.

What would a JAP do during a nuclear holocaust?
Get out her sun reflector.

What's the difference between a JAP and a
freezer?
You have to plug in a freezer.

What does a JAP say as she's reaching orgasm?
"Mom, I've got to hang up now."

What's the difference between a hooker and a
JAP?
A hooker will blow you; a JAP will blow your
mind.

What's the first thing a JAP does with her
asshole in the morning?
Sends him off to work.

Did you hear about the terrible new disease that afflicts JAP?
It's called MAIDS.

How do you give a JAP an orgasm?
Shout, "Charge it to Daddy!"

What makes a JAP different from other wives?
She can dish it out, but she can't cook it.

Why did the JAP wear a two-piece bathing suit?
To separate the meat from the fish.

What does the JAP do before she goes to the plastic surgeon's office?
Pick her nose.

Why do you give a JAP her Chanukah present on Labor Day?
To give her time to exchange it.

How does a JAP know it's time for marriage?
When she picks out a silver pattern.

Why do JAPs like wonton soup?
Because wonton backward spells "not now."

How did the JAP commit suicide?
She piled up all her clothes and jumped.

What do you get when you cross an elephant
and a JAP?
The world's most expensive nose job.

Why won't a JAP eat soybeans?
Soybeans are a meat substitute.

Did you hear that JAPs really don't care for a
man's company?
Unless he owns it.

What does a JAP pledge on her wedding day?
To make a man happy—even if it takes every dollar he has.

What do JAPs do when they lose interest in sex?
They get married.

One JAP met another outside the mall. The second woman asked, "What are you doing these days?"

The first JAP replied, "I'm looking for a new dishwasher."

"What happened to your old one?"

"I divorced him last month."

How can you tell a woman is a JAP?
She's the one eating the banana sideways.

What's long and hard for a man that really excites a JAP?
The road to success.

What's the sexiest four-letter word to a JAP?
Cash.

What do you get when you cross a Jap and a JAP?
An Orienta.

How can you find out what a JAP really thinks of you?
Marry her.

What's the worst thing for a JAP about having a colostomy?
Finding shoes to match the bag.

CHAPTER 2

GREAT JOKES ABOUT JEWISH MARRIAGES

Mel Goldstein's lawyer walked into his office. Goldstein asked, "To what do I owe the honor of this visit?"

"I'm afraid I've got some bad news for you."

"What is it?"

"Your wife got her hands on a picture that's worth at least a million bucks."

Goldstein asked, "That's bad? It sounds terrific."

"Wait," his lawyer continued. "It's a picture of you and your secretary."

Saul and Jacob were having lunch at the country club when Saul complained, "My wife's the worst driver in the world."

"How bad is she?" Jacob asked.

"Let me put it this way," Saul replied. "If she were an Arab, she'd come home with a dented camel."

Why do Jewish husbands die young?
They want to.

Why is a Jewish husband's sex life different from a WASP's?
When he says, "Let's eat out," they go to a restaurant.

Did you hear about the Jewish husband whose wife died during sex?
Three and a half weeks later, he noticed.

Why did the Jewish man divorce his wife and get a dog?
The license was cheaper, the dog didn't have a mother, and it already had a fur coat.

How do you know a Jewish woman's addicted to credit cards?
When she pays cash, she signs the dollar bills.

Harvey Feldstein couldn't sleep one night, so he decided to go downstairs for a snack. When he turned on the light, he was startled to see a burglar entering the back door.

Noticing the panicked look on his face, the burglar said, "I'm not going to hurt you. I just want all your money."

Feldstein immediately rushed forward, yanked away the burglar's flashlight, grabbed him by the collar, shoved him in a closet, locked the door, and called police.

Later, a neighbor who came over when police arrived said to Feldstein, "Harvey, I can't believe you're such a hero."

Feldstein shrugged. "Who's a hero? When the bum told me he wanted all my money, I realized he wasn't any different from my wife."

A Jewish woman was having lunch with a friend when the friend asked, "How's your diet going?"

The first woman grumbled. "I went to that new diet doctor. He told me that every time I make love, I lose three hundred calories."

"That's terrific."

"Not when you're married to Irving. I figure I've lost an average of fifty calories a year."

What's the official term for a Jewish ex-wife? "Plaintiff."

Why didn't the Jewish man ever take his wife to dinner?
He made it a rule never to go out with married women.

A friend came up to Melvin Schwartz a few months after his marriage and asked, "How's married life?"

Schwartz grimaced. "Not so hot."

"What's wrong? Having a little trouble getting Hannah in the sack?"

"Trouble?" Schwartz said sarcastically. "If she died, I don't think I could identify the body."

What's a fifty-fifty settlement in a Jewish divorce?
The wife gets half, and her lawyer gets half.

How does a Jewish wife dress to please her husband?
In last year's clothes.

The clock read 3:00 A.M. when Mrs. Stein suddenly woke her husband, whispering, "Harry, there's a burglar in my dressing room. Go stop him."

Mr. Stein sat up and said, " Are you crazy? What if he's got a gun?"

"So what?" his wife replied. "My jewelry's not insured, but you are."

Sophie Feinstein confided in her girlfriend, "I've decided to break off my engagement with Myron."

"Why?"

"My feelings for him have changed," Sophie replied.

The girlfriend pointed to Sophie's hand and remarked, "But you're still wearing his diamond ring."

Sophie said, "My feelings toward the diamond ring haven't changed."

Why is a Jewish wife like a Thanksgiving turkey? Her husband can only stuff her once a year.

Myron Perlman came home one night and presented his wife with a diamond necklace for their anniversary. His wife said, "It's beautiful, Myron, but I asked you for a Mercedes."

"I know," her husband replied. "But I don't know where to buy an imitation Mercedes."

The Steins had been seeing a marriage therapist, and today Mrs. Stein had a session alone. Taking the opportunity to explore private matters, the therapist asked, "Now tell me, Mrs. Stein, what is your husband's expression when you're having sex?"

She thought for a moment, then replied, "He's usually all flushed and breathing hard. One time, though, he was so angry his teeth were clenched."

"Aha," the therapist said. "And when was that?"

"The time he peeked through the bedroom window."

Why did the Jewish husband learn to lie with a straight face?
So he could lie with a curved body.

What's alimony to a Jewish husband?
Bounty on the mutiny.

What's does alimony mean to a Jewish husband?
He doesn't get screwed until the marriage is over.

Why are there so many unhappy Jewish marriages?
Jewish women get all excited about nothing—then marry him.

Did you hear that Jewish husbands always have the last word?
It's usually, "Yes, dear."

The Jewish couple were in the honeymoon suite consummating their marriage. After a while, he rolled off and leaned back against the pillow. Then she reached over and slapped him in the face.

"What's that for?" he demanded.

"That's for being a lousy lover," she said.

He leaned over and smacked her hard.

"What's that for?" she yelled.

"For knowing the difference," he said.

The couple was arguing. Mrs. Weinstock shouted, "Murray, what would you say if I told you I was sleeping with your best friend?"

Murray responded, "I'd say you were a lesbian."

Do Jewish husbands talk to their wives after sex?

Yes, if there's a telephone handy.

Murray Goldstein returned home from a garment industry convention in Miami. His vice-president walked into his office and said, "Murray, you look terrible. Are you sick or something?"

"No," Murray said. "It's a long story."

"So tell it."

"Well, the first night I get into the hotel and go down to sit by the pool. This gorgeous blonde sits down on the lounger next to me. Turns out she's a buyer in the Midwest who really likes our stuff. One thing leads to another, and we're back in my room fucking our brains out."

"What's wrong with that?"

"Nothing. But afterward, the blonde sits up in bed and starts crying her eyes out. Turns out she's married and has twin babies at home. Her crying gets me thinking about Sylvia and the kids, and I start bawling."

"But Murray," his vice-president said, "that was over two weeks ago. Why are your eyes so red?"

"If you cried your heart out three times a day for two weeks, you'd look like shit, too."

How do you describe a Jewish romance?
The cooing stops after their wedding day, but the billing goes on forever.

The Jewish husband tried to talk his wife into oral sex for years, but she wouldn't yield. Finally she told him, "I might, as long as I don't have to taste that yicky stuff."

Gleeful, the husband went out to buy a box of condoms. He put one on, climbed into bed, and asked her to suck him. But she grimaced and said, "How do I know what that's made of? What if it's made of pork bladder?"

The husband was disappointed. But he went out to a Jewish specialty store and returned with a small box. Triumphantly, he pulled out a condom. When he put it on, the word "kosher" could be clearly read on the side. "Now you can blow me," he said to his wife.

She glared at him. "How dare you put words in my mouth?" she screamed.

When does it get really hot in a Jewish bedroom? When the air conditioner breaks down.

The Jewish wife yelled at her husband, "I had to marry you to find out how stupid you are."

He replied, "You should have known how stupid I was the minute I asked you."

What do you call an independently wealthy Jewish woman?
A divorcée.

How does a Jewish woman lose weight?
She carries around a picture of her husband, naked.

The Jewish husband complained to his wife, "This fish tastes awful."

"I don't understand," she replied. "I know I burned it a little, but I put suntan lotion on it."

Sol Rubinstein was sitting at lunch with a friend when he said, "You know, women think they're so smart."

"What do you mean?"

"Take my wife," Rubinstein said. "I overheard her talking on the phone to her girlfriends. She was saying that I don't know that the only time she lets me sleep with her is when she's trying to get pregnant."

Rubinstein got such a kick from this that he started doubling over with laughter.

"I don't see what's so funny, Sol," his friend said. "I'd be pissed as hell."

"Why get mad?" Sol replied. "She doesn't know that I had a vasectomy."

"Why didn't I listen to Mother?" Mrs. Stein screamed. "She pleaded with me not to marry you!"

"She said that?" Stein asked.

"Of course she did."

"Hmmm," Stein mused. "I'm sorry I've misjudged her all these years."

How hard was it for a Jewish husband to get laid?
He had to get sentenced to prison to get conjugal visits.

Harold got down and his hands and knees to propose to the daughter of his boss, the owner of the garment company. He handed her a ring and said, "Darling, I love you more than life itself. Please take this ring and say you'll be mine. I've saved for months for this ring, and it only has one small flaw."

The girl stared at the ring, then said, "In this diamond, there's no room for a flaw."

Mrs. Broffman rushed into the dining room where her husband was having breakfast and shouted, "Irving, Irving. The maid stole two of our towels. I want her arrested."

"Wait a second," Irving replied. "Which towels did she steal?"

"The white and blue ones. You now, the ones we got from that hotel in Miami Beach."

What's a Jewish husband's idea of safe sex?
His wife is in Miami Beach.

Irving and Sol were having coffee when Irving said, "You know, sex with my wife is like the Fourth of July."

"You mean, fireworks and bright lights?"

"Nah," Irving replied. "I mean once a year."

Sheldon was on top of his wife, pumping away, when she complained. "Can't you get this over with?"

"Sorry," he replied. "I just can't think of anybody."

Mort was sitting in the diner complaining, "I'm so horny all the time, and my wife lets me on top of her about once in a blue moon."

"So take a cold shower," his friend said.

"I've taken so many cold showers," Mort said, "that now I get a hard-on whenever it rains."

Two men were talking outside the temple when one complained, "My wife will use any excuse not to have sex—she got her hair done, she's got a headache, it's her time of month— the list is endless."

The other man grimaced. "Yeah, well, my wife goes her one better."

"How's that?"

"She told me last night she was giving up sex for Lent."

Why did the Jewish man insist that he be buried at sea?
Because his wife told him she would dance on his grave.

When should a Jewish husband be suspicious of his wife?
She calls in a gardener to fertilize her bush.

How did the Jewish guy know his wife was going to file for divorce?
She bought towels that read "Hers" and "Hers Soon."

The Jewish husband came into the bathroom one morning as his wife stepped out of the shower. He grabbed her buttocks with both hands, squeezed, then said, "You know, if you firmed these up, you wouldn't have to keep wearing a girdle."

Her feelings were hurt, and she refused to talk to him for a week. A few days afterward, she was in the shower when he reached in the door, grabbed one of her tits, and said, "You know, if you firmed these up, you wouldn't have to keep wearing a bra."

Furious, she went to her mother's house for two weeks. The day she returned home, she saw her husband getting out of the shower. She reached out, grabbed his dick, and said, "You know, if you could firm this up, I wouldn't have to keep using the gardener."

Bernie Solomon owned a large delicatessen for years. Then, suddenly, he started to have this overwhelming obsession to stick his penis in the pickle slicer. He made an appointment with a shrink and explained his problem.

The shrink explained, "This is what we call obsessive-compulsive behavior. The best way to overcome the problem is to completely remove yourself from temptation."

"I can't do that, doc," Bernie said. "It's my livelihood. My family would starve."

"Then you have to directly confront temptation. As painful as it may be if you give in, you will finally be free."

Bernie nodded and left. The psychiatrist was shocked to see him walking back in the office two days later. Bernie sat down and said, "Doc, I took your advice and I finally stuck my penis in the pickle slicer?"

"And what happened?"

"My wife walked in, and now she's filing for divorce."

What's the difference between a Jewish couple's first honeymoon and their second honeymoon? On the second, he goes in the bathroom and cries.

The obstetrician was washing up after the delivery when Mr. Levine came bursting into the room and demanded, "Doctor, are you sure that's my baby out there?"

"Of course. What's the problem?"

Levine said, "That baby has red hair. But both my wife and myself have black hair."

"Hmmm . . ." The physician pondered for a moment. Then he asked, "How often do you and your wife have sex?"

Levine turned bright red. "Well, my wife doesn't like it much. I'm afraid we haven't screwed since she got pregnant."

"That explains it," the doctor said. "Rust."

The Jewish wife went in to see a therapist and said, "I've got a big problem doctor. Every time we're in bed and my husband climaxes, he lets out this earsplitting yell."

"My dear," the shrink said, "that's completely natural. I don't see what the problem is?"

"The problem is," she complained, "it wakes me up."

Mort and Rachel's marriage ended in a bitter divorce. They didn't see each other for years until they ran into each other at a party. Mort came up to Rachel and asked, "So how's your new husband?"

"He's wonderful," Rachel said. "Sheldon worships the ground I walk on."

Mort sneered. "And what did he think of your tired, worn-out old pussy?"

"He loved it, especially when he got past the little tired, worn-out part."

Mort and Harry were longtime golf and card-playing buddies. One day, they met in the steam room of the country club. Mort said, "Harry, I have something to tell you. I've been screwing your wife and she's in love with me. But I want to settle this like gentlemen. What do you say we play gin rummy for her?"

Harry said, "That's okay with me. But I'll tell you what—just to keep it interesting, how about playing for a penny a point?"

What's the difference between a Jewish bachelor and a married Jewish man?
The bachelor comes home, sees what's in the refrigerator, and goes to bed. The married man comes home, sees what's in bed, and goes to the refrigerator.

The husband walked into the room and sneered. "Why are you bothering to iron your bra? You don't have anything to put in it?"
"I iron your shorts, don't I?" his wife replied.

Sol went to see the doctor one day and said, "You've got to help me. I need something so that I can get it up for my wife."
The doctor consulted his medical books, then gave Sol a pill to swallow. Unfortunately, Sol's wife wasn't home when he got there. Needing relief, he had to masturbate.

The next day, the doctor called and heard the story. He said, "Sol, you didn't have to beat off. There are other women around."

Sol said, "For other women, I don't need a pill."

What's the second shortest book in the world?
The Jewish Wife's Household Hints.

Why does it take a Jewish wife a little while before her new husband really enjoys their meals?
Finding a good restaurant in a new neighborhood takes time.

What's the best thing about Jewish wives?
They make excellent husbands.

Did you hear about the Jewish husband who arranged plastic surgery for his wife?
He cut up her credit cards.

A co-worker arrived at Mel Abromowitz's house. When they were alone in his study, the co-worker asked, "Was that your wife who opened the door?"

Mel said, "You think I'd hire a maid that ugly?"

What's a monologue?
A conversation between a Jewish wife and her husband.

The Jewish woman wrote a letter to her estranged husband that read:

My dearest darling,
I have come to realize that you are right. I spent far too much time nagging and complaining about every little thing. I neglected the housework and spent far too much money on clothing and dining out. Finally, I miss you and I want you in my bed. Please come home tonight so I can show you how much I care.

P.S. Congratulations on winning the lottery.

Why did the ambitious WASP female lawyer
marry Sol Weinstein?
She was told that she'd get rich quicker if she
had a little Jew in her.

CHAPTER 3

GREAT JEWISH JOKES ABOUT MONEY AND BUSINESS

A guy walked into a bar, obviously steaming. A friend walked up and asked, "Jerry, what's wrong?"

"It's Goldberg, my fucking doctor," Jerry swore. "That bastard's bills are driving me to the poorhouse."

"His bills are high?"

"Are you kidding?" Jerry replied. "Every time Goldberg sits down to make out a bill, the burglar alarm goes off."

The furniture salesman cornered Weinberg and his wife and gave them his big pitch about the new living-room set they'd been looking at. The salesman concluded, "One more thing. You only put down a fifty-dollar deposit, then you don't pay a cent for six months."

Weinberg grunted, then turned to his wife and said, "Let's get going. He's heard about us."

A company president decides he needs a new building, so he calls some contractors in to submit bids. The first guy he talks to is Polish.

"You've had a chance to look at the plans," he says. "How much will it cost to build?"

"Two million," replies the Polish contractor. "One million for materials, one million for labor."

The company president thanks the Pole and calls in an Italian contractor.

The Italian's bid is four million.

"How would you break that down?" the company president asks.

"Two million for materials, two million for labor," the Italian replies.

The company president dismisses him, then calls in the third man, a Jewish contractor.

"How much are you bidding?" the president asks.

"Six million."

"Six million? That's very high. How do you break that down?"

"It's simple," says the Jewish contractor. "Two million for me, two million for you, and two million for the Polack."

Cohen and Stein were in the garment business, and they were having their worst year ever. Month after month, ten thousand Madras jackets sat on their racks, and their creditors were closing in like wolves. But just as they were about ready to end it all, the door opened one day and a man announced, "I'm here on a buying trip from Australia. You blokes wouldn't happen to have any Madras jackets, would you?"

Cohen looked at Stein, then said, "Maybe we can dig up a few, if the price is right."

After a couple hours of negotiation, the Australian agreed to buy all ten thousand Madras jackets at a very handsome price.

But just as he was about to leave, he added, "I've got to get home-office approval on this purchase. Today's Monday. If you don't get a cable from me by the end of the week, the deal is final."

For the next four days, Cohen and Stein paced back and forth in the office, wincing each time they thought they heard footsteps outside the door. They thought they were home free as the clock struck four on Friday afternoon.

Suddenly there was a knock at the door and a voice called out, "Western Union." Stein felt so weak he collapsed into a chair. Cohen, his face white, went to the door.

A few long minutes passed. Then Cohen burst into the room, shouting, "Great news! Your sister's dead!"

A Jewish businessman named Feldstein arrived at the Pearly Gates at the same time as a black dude from Harlem. St. Peter greeted the pair, then said, "Welcome to heaven. We're so happy to have you here that I'm allowed to give you anything you want."

The black guy thought a minute, then said, "I wants a million dollars."

Instantly, a million dollars appeared in the dude's hands.

He walked through the gates smiling.

St. Peter turned to Feldstein and said, "Now, my friend, what is your wish."

Feldstein said, "I'll need twenty dollars in fake jewelry. And ten minutes alone with the black fellow."

What do you call the Jewish Mafia?
The Kosher Nostra.

How can you tell if a limousine is owned by a Jew?
There's a pay phone in the backseat.

Did you hear about the Jewish Santa Claus?
He comes down the chimney, wakes the kids,
then says, "Hey, you wanna buy some toys
cheap?"

What do you get when you cross a Jew and a
Mexican?
A migrant lawyer.

How do Jews celebrate Christmas?
They put a parking meter on the roof.

A wealthy American Jew stood at the famous
Wailing Wall, pleading, "Please, God. Send
me a million dollars to pay off my bank note.
Please, God. Please."

While he continued to plead, a shabbily dressed
man came up beside him and started to shriek,
"God, give me twenty dollars. Give me twenty
dollars."

The American turned to the man next to him,
grabbed him by the lapels, and shouted, "Shut
up. I'm talking big business here."

Jules Finkelstein, owner of a garment business, took his employees out for their annual lunch. After the meal, he gave his annual inspirational speech, during which he remarked, "There are hundreds of ways to make a fortune, but only one honest way."

"And what's that?" one of his salesman asked.

Finkelstein shrugged. "How should I know?"

The salesman was trying to close a big sale with Harvey Weinberg, a vice-president of a major electronics firm. As negotiations came down to the wire, the salesman mentioned that he'd toss in a brand-new Mercedes if the deal was signed.

Weinberg was indignant. "So who do you think you're dealing with, some slimy politician? I can't accept a bribe."

The salesman said, "Well, in that case, we won't make it a gift. Suppose I sell you the Mercedes for a hundred dollars."

"In that case," Weinberg replied, "I'll take two."

What's the definition of a dumb Jewish businessman?
A guy who sets up shop in a fireproof building.

Did you hear about the Jewish guy who's been riding the bus for twelve years?
The sign on the door says, "Pay as you leave."

An Irishman, a Polack, and a WASP were attending the funeral of a co-worker. They were standing by the coffin when the Irishman said, "Barney died before I could pay him back the twenty dollars I owe him." Then he took a twenty out of his wallet and put it in the casket.

The Polack said, "That reminds me, I owed Barney twenty, too." He also deposited the bill beside the first.

The WASP chuckled to himself, then said, "Yes, I happened to owe Barney yet another twenty dollars." Then he pulled out his checkbook, wrote a check to cash for sixty dollars, and replaced the two twenties with the check.

Three days later, the WASP discovered that the check had been cashed. The funeral director was Jewish.

Sam Cohen, owner of a big garment company, was getting divorced from his wife. Her attorney came into to see him and said, "Sadie is entitled to half of all you've earned during your marriage. We calculate that is worth five million dollars."

Sam shrugged and said, "Sorry, all I can legally give her is 10 percent, or five hundred thousand."

"What happened to the rest of it?" the attorney asked.

"I've written 90 percent of her off for depreciation," Cohen replied.

Joshua Feldstein, a young investment banker, came into the Wall Street bar late one night, ordered a double scotch on the rocks, then downed it in a gulp. A friend came over, noticed Joshua was pale, then asked, "Josh, what's wrong? Bad day in the markets?"

"No," Feldstein replied. "It's what happened after work. I was walking down a nearly empty street when this young girl came up to me and asked for a handout. It was freezing, but she had on a light sweater, a sleeveless blouse, and a short skirt. She was shaking, and she told me she hadn't eaten for days."

"That sounds so depressing," the friend said.

"Yeah," Feldstein said. "I'll tell you, I could barely hold back the tears while I was fucking her."

Cohen was sitting in his office when the black security guard rushed in and said, "Mista Cone, Mista Cone, some dude done get into your Caddy and tries to steal it."

Cohen leaped to his feet. "Did you try to stop him?"

"No, suh," the guard replied. "But I didst get the license plate number."

The old man hobbled into Dr. Fromstein's office and complained, "Doctor, I can't pee."

Fromstein asked, "How old are you?"

"I'm eighty-nine."

"Well," said the doctor, "haven't you peed enough?"

Mrs. Saperstein went to the doctor's office, entered the examining room, and put on a robe. The doctor walked in and said, "So, Mrs. Saperstein, what seems to be the trouble?"

Immediately, the Jewish woman sat up, grabbed her clothes, and stormed toward the door.

"What's the problem?" the doctor asked.

"All those years in medical school," Mrs. Saperstein said, "and you want me to make the diagnosis?"

Why are Jewish businessmen so hard on their employees?
To turn the wheels of progress, you need a crank.

Why did the garment executive decide to produce a corduroy pillow?
He wanted to make head lines.

The Jewish man walked into a shrink's office and said, "Doctor, I have this terrible inferiority complex because my penis is so short."
"Let me see the problem," the shrink said.
The man dropped his pants.
The shrink said, "I wouldn't let a little thing like that bother you."

What's the difference between a Jewish lawyer and a vulture?
A Jewish lawyer can take off his wing tips.

Attorney Shellstein was explaining his fee structure to a prospective client. "Mrs. Wolff," he said, "if we file suit and we lose, I get absolutely nothing."

"And what if we win?"

"Then," the lawyer replied, "you end up with nothing."

After being arrested for embezzlement, Sol Drapowitz called his second cousin, who was a lawyer. His cousin came to see him at the jail and asked, "So tell me, did you really take the money."

Sol replied, "I've got almost two million dollars buried in a box underneath my rose garden."

The attorney grinned. "Sol, you'll never go to jail with that kind of money."

The attorney was right. When Sol went to jail, he didn't have a cent left.

Did you hear that a Jewish group bought Irving Trust?
It's now called Trust Irving.

Why did the Jewish guy move from California to New York?
He wanted to get paid three hours earlier.

What's the difference between a rich Jew and a poor Jew?
A poor Jew has to wash his own Cadillac.

How does a camera store know a customer is Jewish?
When he asks if he can rent flash bulbs.

Did you hear about the Jewish guy who went to Atlantic City?
He was too cheap to play roulette, so he bet mentally—and lost his mind.

The wife was removing some old clothes from the closet when she reached into the pocket of a pair of slacks and found a ticket for a dress that she'd taken to the tailor's for alterations nearly four years before. Later that day, she walked into Cohen's Tailor Shop and handed the ticket to the proprietor.

He looked at the ticket, then said, "Okay, lady, it'll be ready next Friday."

Sydney Dobkin spent days on end at his dying father's beside. Concerned about his health and mental state, his aunt Sophie decided that what he needed was to get his mind off the tragedy. She fixed him up with the beautiful young daughter of a friend of hers.

The two went out to dinner. Sydney couldn't resist talking about his father. "You know," he said, "in just a few short days I'll inherit my father's wholesale business. I'll be worth at least five million dollars."

Sympathetically, the young Jewish girl took his hand. After dinner, she went home with him, and the next day she became his stepmother.

Why don't Jews like sex?
Because it's a business where you start out on top and end up at the bottom.

What's the most popular game show among Jews?
"The Price Is Right."

A fifty-year-old man is sitting in the psychiatrist's office. A nurse brings in his folder, then tells the doctor, "His driver's license says he's Irving Goldberg. But he insists he's Napoleon Bonaparte."

The psychiatrist nods, turns to the man, and says, "What can I do for you, sir?"

"What could you do for me?" the man says. "I have the most powerful armies in Europe, I have wealth beyond counting, and my palace is the most beautiful in the world."

"Then why are you here?" the shrink asks.

"It's my wife," the man says. "She's got this problem. She insists her name is Mrs. Goldberg."

In the middle of a dinner at the temple, Mr. Cohen got up and announced, "I just lost my wallet with five hundred dollars in it. I'll give a fifty-dollar reward to anyone who finds it."

Then a voice from the back said, "I'll give seventy-five."

Two business partners from the garment district were fishing in the Catskills. Suddenly a storm blew in from over the mountains and capsized their boat. Goldberg began to splash helplessly in the water. His partner, Feinstock, clung to a piece of driftwood. He shouted, "Melvin, can you float alone?"

Goldberg sputtered, "I'm drowning, you bastard, and you're talking business."

Young Solomon Goldstein had just started as a salesman in his father's clothing store. He'd been waiting on a customer when he came back into his father's office and said, "The customer, he wants to know if the unshrinkable wool suits will ever shrink?"

His father asked, "How does the suit fit him?"

"It's too large."

"Then tell him it will shrink."

How does a Jew commit suicide?
He hangs from the rafters with one hand and chokes himself with the other to save the cost of rope.

Mrs. Silverstein went in for a routine checkup, so she was surprised when Dr. Cohen called her into the office and said, "I'm afraid you need major surgery. We're sending you directly to the hospital."

"Oh, no," she said. "Is this necessary?"

"Vital," the physician said. "And I'm sorry to inform you that the surgical procedures will cost sixty thousand dollars.

Mrs. Silverstein was shaken. "I don't have that kind of money."

The doctor said, "You can pay me on the installment plan."

"You mean, like buying a car?"

"Yes, I am," the doctor replied.

A woman stormed into the Jewish deli and said, "I'm disgusted. I bought a loaf of raisin bread this morning. When I got it home and sliced it, I found two cockroaches inside."

The owner shrugged. "So what's the problem, lady? Bring back the roaches and I'll give you two raisins."

Did you hear about the new delicatessen for Christians only?
It's called, "Goys 'R Us."

Marvin Saperstein owned a Jewish deli in New York. One year he was called in by the IRS for an audit. The agent reviewed his records, then said, "Mr. Saperstein, I understand most of your deductions for foodstuffs, rent, utilities, labor, paper products, etc. But you sell sandwiches and beverages. How come you deducted twelve trips to Israel?"

Saperstein shrugged. "We deliver."

The man stormed into the clothing store and shouted at Hyman Levine, "You told me this suit was all wool. So why does it have this label that says '100 percent polyester'?"

Levine said, "We put that in there to fool the moths."

Morris Bernstein had recently brought his young son into the business and was in the process of teaching him the ropes. Some time later, Bernstein came back into the stockroom where his son worked, pulled him aside, and said, "Today we're going to talk about ethics. Nothing is more important in business than ethics."

"So talk," the son said.

"A few minutes ago, an old lady came in to buy a month's groceries. She lives on Social

Security and the check came today. I add up all the stuff and she gives me a fifty-dollar bill."

"I don't understand the problem," the son said.

"Listen. After she's gone, I discover that she actually gave me two fifties that were stuck together. Now, here's the ethical problem—do I tell my partner or not?"

A Jew and an Irishman were having lunch in a very fancy restaurant. When the bill came, the Jewish fellow announced, "I'll take it."

The next day, the headline said, "Irish Ventriloquist Killed in Restaurant."

An Irishman, an Italian, and a Jew were sitting around a table talking about what they would do if they woke up one morning with a million dollars. The Irishman said, "I'd go out every morning for thirty days and buy myself a case of the finest whiskey in the world."

The Italian remarked, "I'd spend a month in the best whorehouse in the world, taking a different girl every day."

The Jew listened and said, "I'd go back to sleep and dream about waking up with another million dollars."

A man on crutches hobbled up to a Jewish businessman and said, "Please, sir, can you help me. I just lost a leg."

The Jew looked at him and said, "I'm busy. Why don't you put an ad in the paper?"

Mort Berkowitz came to see his best friend Sol and said, "I have a terrible dilemma. I can't decide whether to marry the incredibly wealthy widow my mother introduced to me or the beautiful waitress that I really love. What should I do?"

Sol said, "That's easy. You need to do two things. First, nothing is more important than love, so you should elope with the waitress tonight."

"Thank you," Mort said. "I'll leave right now. But what's the second thing?"

"Give me the address of the widow."

The editor of *The New York Times* received this letter:

Dear Sir,

As a Zionist and a Jew I must protest your scandalous coverage of the legitimate efforts of the state of Israel to protect itself against Palestinian terrorism.

I demand that you cease printing lies about acts of brutality committed by Israeli soldiers. If you don't, I shall be forced to stop borrowing a copy of your newspaper every day.

Sheldon Markowitz was sitting in the doctor's office when the physician came in to report, "The tests on the urine sample you submitted were completely negative. You've got a clean bill of health."

"Great," Sheldon said. "Can I use your phone for a moment?"

The doctor nodded.

Sheldon dialed, then said, "Honey, great news. You, the kids, your mother, and I are all completely healthy."

How did the Grand Canyon come into being? A Jewish explorer dropped a gold piece.

How did the cops catch the Jewish pervert? He made all his obscene phone calls collect.

How many Jewish businessmen does it take to change a light bulb?
Three. One to screw in the bulb and two to kick the chair out from under him.

Mr. Weinstock walked into a lawyer's office and said, "I'll hire you if you tell me that you can absolutely win the case."

The attorney said, "Tell me the facts."

Weinstock went on for half an hour, until he'd concluded the argument. The attorney thought for only a moment. Then he said, "No problem, We'll win easily. It's an open-and-shut case."

Weinstock groaned. "I'm ruined," he said.

"What's the problem?"

"I just told you my partner's side of the story."

The funeral for the extremely wealthy Jewish industrialist was over, and one mourner was on the sidewalk, sobbing hysterically. Finally, a passerby came up to console him. "I'm so sorry for your loss," the man said. "What was your relation to the deceased?"

"None whatsoever," the man sobbed. "That's why I'm crying."

What do you get when you cross a Jew and a gypsy?
A chain of empty stores.

How many Jewish lawyers does it take to screw in a light bulb?
Six. One to carry the bulb, and five to do the screwing.

Why did the tribes of Israel wander the desert for forty years?
Somebody dropped a nickel.

Did you hear about the movie called *Altered Suits?*
It's about a Jewish man who takes acid and buys retail.

Did you hear about the new Jewish tire?
It not only stops on a dime, it picks it up.

Sheldon Bernstein was a real-estate broker whose office was across the street from his hated archrival, Jacob Cohen. Bernstein was out inspecting a house one day when he came across an old lamp. He rubbed the lamp, and sure enough, a genie popped out. The genie said, "You are granted three wishes. However, I must tell you that your worst enemy will be granted twice what you wish for."

Sheldon thought for a moment, then said, "I want one billion dollars deposited to my account."

The genie waved his wand, then said, "You have one billion, and your enemy Cohen has two billion."

Bernstein thought for a moment, then wished, "I want a harem of ten of the most beautiful and sexually experienced women in the world."

The wish was granted, but Cohen got a harem of twenty women.

"You have one wish left," the genie said.

Sheldon replied, "I wish that one of my testicles would disappear."

The hooker had just finished a little business in the diamond district, and she popped into one of the streetfront stores to get an appraisal of her new diamond ring. The owner examined it, then said, "Madam, I'm afraid this isn't a real diamond."

"Help," the hooker screamed. "I've been raped!"

Why did the Jew cross the road?
To franchise the other side.

The businessman walked into the Jewish deli, sat down, and ordered a pastrami sandwich. When his meal arrived, he angrily called the owner over and said, "Hey, I ordered this sandwich yesterday and it had three times as much meat."

The Jewish owner shrugged. "Yesterday, you were sitting in the window."

Milt Weinstein walked into the IRS auditor's office and sat down. The auditor said, "I call you in here today to tell you that you should be proud to be an American. And part of that pride should be supporting your country by paying your taxes accurately and cheerfully. What do you say to that?"

Weinstein said, "I'm relieved. I thought you called me in here to demand money."

What's the shortest book in the world?
The Jewish Book of Business Ethics.

Three Jewish businessmen were lamenting the fact that business had been so lousy. "I was losing money for months," one said. "Fortunately, I had a fire and collected two hundred and fifty thousand in insurance."

The second one said, "You think you had it bad? The creditors were at my door. Fortunately, a flood destroyed my business and I collected five hundred thousand from insurance."

The third one asked, "How do you start a flood?"

It was nearly two o'clock in the morning when a passerby noticed smoke coming from a window of the Cohen Garment Company. He dashed inside to see a mound of boxes in flame. He also noticed that the company president was there, filling a bucket from a large tank, dashing frantically over to the fire, dousing the flames with the contents of the bucket, then dashing back to the tank. The passerby went up and said, "Mr. Cohen. We'd better call the fire department. What you're doing doesn't seem to help at all?"

"Of course it helps," Cohen snapped. "It's gasoline."

Sol Steinberg was driving down the street with his family when they saw a sign on an evangelical Christian church that said, "Give your life to Jesus—$500 reward to converts."

The deal was too good to pass up, so Steinberg pulled over to the church, rushed inside, converted to Christianity, and collected his reward. When he got back in the car, his wife said, "That's a lot of money. I want a fur coat."

His daughter chimed in, "I want diamond earrings."

His son said, "I need a new bike."

Steinberg shook his head sadly. "It's always the same story. We Gentiles get some money, you Jews want to take it away."

The collection agency, desperate to collect something on all its delinquent accounts in the garment business, broke down and hired Sam Melwitz, its first Jewish employee. The owner of the agency sent him out the first day, warning him that he would be fired if he came back empty-handed.

To his shock, Melwitz came back with over fifty thousand dollars. He told his boss, "I got the money from Cohen, from Stein, from Markowitz—"

His boss interrupted. "I don't understand. We've been hounding those people for years. What did you do?"

"Simple," the Jewish man replied. "I told all of them if they didn't give me the money, I'd tell all their other creditors that they paid us."

What do you call a Jewish company that's losing ten thousand dollars a month?
A surefire proposition.

What's a CPA?
A Jewish boy who stutters and can't stand the sight of blood.

Why were the police called to the movie theater?
Two Jews were trying to get in on one ticket, on grounds that they were half-brothers.

How does a Jewish businessman read the *Wall Street Journal*?
Over another businessman's shoulder.

How can you tell a Jewish businessman's room? He's saved all his boyhood toys for his second childhood.

What did the Jewish man give his parents for their fiftieth wedding anniversary? Goldfish.

What's the best precaution before going to a Jewish dentist? Count your money before he gives you the gas.

Why are there so many more Jewish dentists than Jewish auto mechanics? People have thirty-two teeth, but only two cars.

How did Jews get a reputation for being such skillful afterdinner speakers? They're always on the telephone when the check arrives.

Why wouldn't the Jewish couple let their youngest daughter get married?
The rice was too dirty after the first three daughters' weddings.

CHAPTER 4

GREAT ETHNIC JOKES ABOUT JEWS

What's a Jewish pervert?
A guy who wants to go into his mother's business.

How do you wash genitals?
The same way you wash Jews.

The Jewish woman and the black man had a little boy. One day, the boy came home from school obviously distressed. "What's wrong?" his mother asked.

"I've gotta know if I'm more Jewish or more black," the boy said.

"That's a tough one, son," the mother said. "Why don't you ask your father."

The little boy waited until Dad came home from work. When he popped the question, his father demanded to be told why he wanted to know.

"You see, Freddy down the street has a bike to sell. I don't know whether to bargain him down or just wait until dark and steal it."

What's the difference between karate and judo? Karate is a martial art. Jew dough is what you use to make bagels.

During World War II, Adolf Hitler consulted a clairvoyant to find out what the future held. The clairvoyant looked into a crystal ball and said, "Mein Führer, I see that you are going to die on a Jewish holiday."

The Führer exploded. "Impossible."

The clairvoyant shrugged. "That is what my vision said."

Hitler demanded, "If it's true, what Jewish holiday will it be?"

"Mein Führer," the clairvoyant answered, "any day you die will be a Jewish holiday."

Two black dudes were walking by a synagogue on Rosh Hashanah when they heard the long, plaintive wail of the ram's horn.

"What's that?" asked the first dude.

"I don't know," the second black said.

Just then a Jewish man who'd been walking behind them tapped him on the shoulder and explained, "You've just heard the Jews blowing their shofar."

"Wow!" exclaimed the first black guy. "You people sure done know how to treat your help."

The strong man at the state fair picked up a grapefruit in one giant hand, then squeezed. Juice poured out until the grapefruit appeared to be bone dry. The barker then announced, "Any man that can get another drop from that grapefruit wins five hundred dollars."

Among the audience were several hulks from the football team at the state university. They stepped forward, then failed. Next, a group of burly construction workers took their turns with the grapefruit, but they came up dry. Two professional wrestlers suffered a similar fate.

The barker was just about to go on to the next act when a small, skinny man with thick glasses stepped forward and announced, "I want to try."

The crowd roared with laughter. Shouts of derision filled the tent as the scrawny man walked up to the table and grabbed the grapefruit. But the crowd gasped in amazement as the man squeezed a half glass of juice from the grapefruit.

The barker and the strong man came running up and demanded, "How come a wimp like you can squeeze like that?"

"I'm Jewish."

What's a Jewish car accident?
No damage to the automobile, but everyone inside has whiplash.

Why are the sturdiest chairs always made out of kosher wood?
They never tip.

Why did the Polish policeman let the Jewish criminal go?
He'd heard that Jews eat lox.

Why did the bee wear a yarmulke?
He wanted to make sure no one mistook him for a WASP.

What do you get when you cross an Irishman and a Jew?
A drunk who gets his liquor wholesale.

Meyer Feldstein had a few too many drinks at the convention, and he began to rant and rave about competition from the Japanese. He got so incensed that when he saw an Oriental man, he dashed across the room, smacked the guy in the face, and shouted, "That's for Pearl Harbor!"

The man he'd hit shouted, "You crazy! I'm not Japanese, I'm Korean."

Feldstein shrugged. "Japanese, Chinese, Korean, it's all the same to me."

Feldstein went back to his friends and had another drink. As he took a first sip, the Korean came up behind him and hit him over the head with a wine bottle, shouting, "That's for the *Titanic*!"

Feldstein fell to the floor stunned. But a moment later he'd recovered enough to demand, "You idiot! What do I have do with the *Titanic*?"

The Oriental shrugged. "Goldberg, Greenberg, iceberg—they're all the same to me."

The forty-six-year-old man suffered a major heart attack. He pulled through, but a few days later he was told by his doctor that he only had a few days left unless he had a heart transplant.

The man said to the doctor, "I'm a wealthy man. Find me the absolutely best heart available."

The doctor returned an hour later and said, "I've contacted an organ bank in Texas. They have the heart of man your own age who died in an auto accident. The man was in great physical condition, had very low cholesterol, and no family history of heart disease. You can get this heart for fifty thousand dollars."

The patient said, "That sounds okay, doc. But I'd feel better if you'd check around some more."

An hour later, the doctor returned and announced, "I've got a real find. It's the heart of a college track star who was a perfect human specimen. He never smoked, never drank, ate only organic foods, and trained high up in the mountains where there's no air pollution. This heart is going to cost you five hundred thousand."

The sick man said, "I told you, money is no object. I'll gladly pay the half million. But I want you to check one more time to make sure I'm getting the best."

This time the doctor was gone for two hours. He came back into the room and announced, "It's a miracle, but I found a third heart. The guy was sixty-seven, smoked a dozen cigars a day, never exercised, had a huge pot belly, ate nothing but saturated fat, and had high blood pressure. This heart will cost you one million."

The patient was astounded. "A million dollars? Why in the world is that heart worth a million dollars?"

The doctor replied, "The heart is from a Jewish pawnbroker. It's never been used."

How can you tell a Jewish household?
There are burglar alarms on the garbage cans.

How can you tell if a man walking down the street is Jewish?
He hands out pledges to beggars.

What happened when the funeral home announced a half-price sale?
2,437 Jews committed suicide.

How do we know Christ was Jewish?
At the Last Supper, he insisted on separate checks.

What do Jewish families tell trick-or-treaters on Halloween?
"Your candy's in the mail."

How do you cure a Jewish man who stutters?
Dial Israel and put him on the phone.

What would happen if Santa Claus were Jewish?
Presents would come COD.

What else would happen if Santa Claus were Jewish?
You'd find pledges in your stocking.

What's the difference between Jewish in-laws and Jewish outlaws?
Jewish outlaws don't want to live with you.

Why should blacks love Jews?
When was the last time they got hired by somebody poor?

What's the fastest game in the world?
Passing the check at a Jewish country club.

How do you tell a Jewish Ethiopian?
He's the one with the Rolex around his waist.

How do we know the universe is Jewish?
The sun is named Sol.

What's a Jewish bird call?
Cheap, cheap, cheap.

What do you call a group of racist Jews who burn Stars of David on people's lawns?
The Klu Klux Kleins.

Did you hear about the Japanese-Jewish restaurant?
It's called, "So Sue Me."

What's a Jewish cocktail party like?
Lots of whine and cheese.

How do you describe a Jewish cocktail party?
A fete worse than death.

Mort ran into an old friend from Hebrew school who stuttered very badly. Mort asked, "What are you doing these days, Hymie?"

The friend said, "I j-j-just went to the r-r-radio station for an au-au-audition."

"How did you do?" Mort asked.

"F-f-fine," Hymie replied. "But they don't hire J-J-Jews."

What does a black Jew say?
"Slap me five—percent."

What did the doctor say to the Jewish convert
who was awaiting circumcision?
"It won't be long now."

How do you tell a Jewish gangster from an
Italian gangster?
The Jewish gangster's wearing the Italian suit.

Did you hear about the guy who was half-Jewish
and half-Japanese?
He was circumcised at Benny Hannah's.

What's the difference between a Jew and a
black?
About 3,600 years.

What did one mink say to another as they were
about to be taken off to be killed and skinned?
"See you at the temple."

What did Mr. Mink give Mrs. Mink for Christmas?
A full-length Jew.

Why should we be thankful they circumcise Jews?
If they didn't, there'd be no end to those pricks.

Why are synagogues round?
So Jews can't hide in the corner when the collection plate comes around.

Why were Moses' parents so happy?
They not only had fun in bed, they also made a prophet.

What's the difference between a porcupine and a synagogue?
A porcupine has its pricks on the outside.

Feldbaum had ignored his religion all his life, until frail health made him a little nervous. He went to the rabbi for religious instruction so he could be a devout Jew. The rabbi said, "I must ask you some questions so I am sure you are ready to accept our faith. Tell me, have you renounced sin."

"Yes, I have," Feldbaum replied.

"And are you devoted to your family?"

"Yes."

"Good," the rabbi said. "Have you embraced a truthful life of charity and sacrifice?"

"I have," Feldbaum replied.

"One final question. Are you ready to settle all your debts to your fellowmen?"

"Wait a second, rabbi," Feldbaum said angrily. "Now you're talking business, not religion."

What's the difference between a rabbi and a priest?
Priests have lower divorce rates.

A rabbi and an Irish priest happened to sit together on the bus one day. As the motor coach rolled along, the priest turned and said, "I hope you don't mind a question. I know you Jews aren't supposed to eat pork. But you have ever given in to temptation and tasted it?"

The rabbi confessed, "Yes, I admit I've tried a bite a time or two."

They rode for a while in silence. Then the rabbi asked, "Tell me, I know you priests are supposed to be celibate. But have you ever given in to temptation and had intercourse?"

The priest paused for a moment, then said, "I admit I've tried it a time or two."

The rabbi grinned. "Better than pork, isn't it?"

Why did they think Christ was the Messiah? He was the first Jew who was well hung.

The rabbi answered the telephone. An IRS auditor was on the line. He said, "Rabbi, I'm auditing the return of one Sam Cohen, a member of your temple. On last year's return, he deducted a charitable contribution of fifty thousand dollars. I wonder if you could furnish us with a receipt for that donation."

"Not at this moment," the rabbi said. "But I will later, after I give Sam a call."

What's circumcision? A way to separate the mensch from the goys.

One day a priest, a minister, and a rabbi rented a boat and went fishing on a lake. They were on the water for about an hour when the priest announced he had to take a leak. To the amazement of the rabbi, the priest stepped out of the boat and walked across the water to an outhouse on the shore.

Another hour passed. Then the minister said that nature called. He, too, stood up, stepped out of the boat, and walked across the water to the outhouse.

The rabbi thought he had witnessed a miracle of faith. When his bladder filled, he stood up, announced, "Lord, I believe," stepped out of the boat, and promptly sank to the bottom. As the rabbi surfaced, splashing frantically, the priest turned to the minister and said, "Should we tell him about the rocks?"

A local fire department brought a brand-new one-hundred-and-fifty-thousand-dollar fire engine, and they asked the local clergy to bless the new machine. First, the Catholic priest came over, sprinkled holy water on the fire engine, and said a prayer. A Protestant clergyman approached the truck next, placed a Bible in the glove compartment, and said, "Dear Lord, we ask you to bless this truck and the brave men who daily risk death to combat fires." Third came the rabbi, who went up to the truck and snipped two inches off the end of the hose.

The Israelites were waiting anxiously at the foot of the mountain. They were all concerned about Moses, who had been up negotiating with God since dawn. Finally, the prophet came into view. After he'd rested a few minutes, Moses said, "I've got some good news and some bad news. The good news is that I bargained him down from fifteen commandments to ten. The bad news is, adultery is still in."

What did Moses say to God when he was up on the mount?
"You want us to cut off the end of our what?"

What do you do with a worn-out bra?
Use it as a skullcap for Siamese-twin rabbis.

On a trip to Israeli the pope was invited by Prime Minister Perez to play a round of golf. Having never picked up a club, the pope consulted his advisers, who told him, "Call Jack Nicklaus. Make him an honorary cardinal, then tell the prime minister you're sick and he has to play in your place."

"Good idea," His Holiness agreed. He called Nicklaus, who readily agreed. A few days later, the pope eagerly awaited the American's return from the course. But he was disappointed when Cardinal Nicklaus told him he'd lost.

"I can't believe the prime minister beat you," the pope lamented.

"Oh, it wasn't him," Nicklaus replied. "I was beaten by Rabbi Palmer."

The rabbi and the priest were sitting at the head table at the community luncheon when the meal was served. To the great amusement of the priest, the main course turned out to be ham. As the rabbi pushed his plate aside, the priest joked, "Rabbi Cohen, when are you going to be liberal enough to eat ham?"

The rabbi replied, "At your wedding, Father McGuire."

Two Jewish men were passing the window of a Christian religious store. They stopped to look at the display of pictures of the baby Jesus in the manger, Jesus and Mary, and the entire holy family.

"What are those pictures?" one asked the other.

The second explained, "Those are pictures of Jesus and his family. The story goes he was born in a manger when they couldn't get a room in the inn."

The first Jew shook his head. "Just like those guys to waste money on pictures when they can't afford a hotel room."

Old Mel Saperstein keeled over with a heart attack on a downtown street. A priest, seeing the man struggling for his life, decided to administer last rites. He knelt down and said, "My son, do you believe in the Father, the Son, and the Holy Ghost?"

Saperstein lifted his head and said, "What is this? I'm dying, and you're asking me riddles."

How can you tell if a rabbi is sentimental?
He keeps a scrapbook of his clippings.

How religious are Jews?
They turn every store into a temple—they walk around, look at the prices, and shout, "Oh, my God!"

The rabbi and the priest were talking shop one day when the priest bragged, "We Catholic clergymen have excellent chances for promotion. You rabbis have to stay rabbis all your lives."

The rabbi said, "That's not exactly the case. We can get promoted."

"Come on," the priest scoffed. "You can't be bishops?"

"No, better."

"Or cardinals?"

"No, better."

"Pope?"

"No, better."

The irritated priest said, "You're not telling me you can be God."

"Why not," the rabbi said. "One of our boys made it before."

What did the Jewish guy do when he discovered that his girlfriend had a heart of gold?
Ripped it out and sold it.

Two men were standing next to each other at a urinal when one said, "I bet you were born at Mount Sinai Hospital."

"That's right," the second man said.

"And I'll bet that your family called in Dr. Levine to circumcise you."

"How did you guess?" the second man said in astonishment.

"It's not a guess. Dr. Levine always cuts on an angle. And you're pissing on my shoe."

It was time to have the baby circumcised, but the Jewish couple was determined to go bargain hunting. They called one rabbi, who said he charged two hundred dollars. "Too much," they said.

They called a second rabbi, who said he charged a hundred. "Too much," they said.

They decided to do it themselves and grabbed a big knife. A couple of minutes later they looked down and exclaimed, "Too much!"

CHAPTER 5

GREAT JOKES ABOUT JEWISH MOTHERS AND CHILDREN

How many Jewish mothers does it take to screw in a light bulb?

Four. One to screw it in, one to complain that it's being screwed in the wrong way, one to complain about the cost of light bulbs these days, and one to feel guilty that the old one burned out.

The ladies were having tea at the temple and, as usual, were complaining about their children. Finally, the rabbi came up to Mrs. Grossman, who had held the floor for at least ten minutes. He said, "Come, now, Mrs. Grossman. Your children may not be perfect. But you'd have children if you had to do it all over again, wouldn't you?"

"Of course I would," Mrs. Grossman replied. "I just wouldn't have the same ones."

One man was talking to another at the temple. He asked, "So where is that boy of yours?"

"Josh is in college," the second man replied.

"What's he taking?"

The second man grimaced. "Every cent I have."

Why don't Jewish women have any moral qualms about abortion?
They believe life doesn't begin until medical school.

How did the Jewish mother cure her son of bedwetting?
She bought him an electric blanket.

The houselights dimmed after intermission, but instead of the second act the audience heard a grief-stricken theater manager announce, "Ladies and gentleman, I'm very sorry to have to announce that our leading man suffered a fatal heart attack in his dressing room between acts. We're going to have to cancel the rest of the performance."

A stunned silence came over the crowd until an elderly Jewish woman stood and yelled, "Give him an enema!"

"Madam," the theater manager said, "I said the heart attack was fatal."

"Give him an enema!" she shouted again.

The theater manager became perturbed. "I repeat, our leading man is dead. An enema can't possibly help."

The Jewish woman shrugged her shoulders and said, "It can't hurt."

Who was the Virgin Mary?
The only truly happy Jewish mother in history.

Did you hear about the new Jewish Mother's Auto Insurance Company?
They offer a special "My Fault" policy.

A woman walked next door to see her Jewish neighbor, Mrs. Cohen. She found the lady carefully scraping the paint off the living-room wall and collecting the chips in a cup. The woman asked, "Mrs. Cohen, are you going to repaint?"

"No," Mrs. Cohen replied. "We're moving."

Sophie walked into the beauty parlor, obviously wincing in great pain every time she took a step. Her friend Myrna came up to her and said, "Sophie, dear, what's the problem?"

Sophie wailed, "It's these shoes. They're two sizes too small."

"So why don't you buy a new pair?" Myrna asked.

"It's my family," Sophie replied. "That no good husband of mine spent so much time screwing his secretary that his business is going bankrupt. My son, the college boy, calls home and says he's a homosexual. My oldest boy dropped out of medical school to become a musician. And my daughter is so ugly that no one will ever marry her."

Myrna looked puzzled. "So what does all this have to do with your shoes?"

Sophie said, "I wear these all day, then I come home, finally take them off—I feel like I won the lottery."

Why was the Jewish mother dismissed from jury duty?
Before the trial began, she stood up and insisted she was guilty.

Harvey Feldstein dropped his mother off at the cemetery. When he returned to pick her up a few minutes later, he saw tears running down her cheeks. When he asked her what was the matter, all she could do was sob and point to the new headstone on her husband's grave.

Harvey read:

Melvin Feldstein
1918–1989
Here lies a devoted husband
and an honest man.

Harvey turned to his mother and said, "So why are you crying?"

His mother barked, "Can't you see, you idiot? They buried two other people in your father's grave?"

How can you tell if a Jewish kid is rich?
His piggy bank has a vice-president.

The teacher was asking questions about last night's homework. She pointed to little Alvin Schwartz and asked, "Alvin, can you tell us who was president when the Civil War began?"

Alvin stared at her.

The teacher said, "Alvin, did you do your homework last night?"

Alvin stared at her.

The teacher, angry, demanded, "Alvin, answer my question."

Alvin replied, "I'm not answering any questions until you call my lawyer."

The Jewish mother arrived at her bridge club bursting with pride. She announced, "My Melvin graduated from college and got his first job."

Another woman remarked, "I didn't know that. When did he graduate?"

"Eleven years ago," the mother replied.

Mel thought his was doing his friend Arthur a favor when he introduced him to a very beautiful girl from the temple. To Mel's great surprise, he saw Arthur out on the town the next week with the girl's mother. Mel waited until his friend went to the bathroom, then hurried after him.

When they were inside the room, Mel said, "You must be crazy. I introduce you to a gorgeous young thing, and you're dating a Jewish mother."

"What's so crazy?" Arthur asked. "She fixes me three meals a day, she doesn't run around with other guys, and when I take off my clothes to make love, she washes and irons them before I put them back on."

Murray Felder called the doctor one night and said, "It's my mother, doc. I think you ought to see her."

"Now, Murray," the doctor said. "Your mother's been a hypochondriac for sixty-nine years. She always thinks she's sick."

"I know," the son replied. "But now she thinks she's dead."

Her daughter, an anthropologist, had been on an expedition deep in the African jungle for over two years. So her Jewish mother was estatic when she received a cable announcing that her daughter was not only coming home, but was also engaged to the man of her dreams.

The mother called all of her friends and relatives, and a party of nearly eighty people thronged the airport gate. But the people gasped loudly when they saw the daughter emerging from the plane holding the hand of a seven-foot-tall black man dressed in a loincloth, holding a spear, and wearing a bone through his nose.

The mother stood in shocked silence for a moment, then rushed up to her daughter and said, "Don't you ever listen? All your life, I said marry a rich doctor, not a witch doctor!"

How did the Jewish kid suspect his parents didn't love him?
His father hired twelve lawyers to find a loophole in his birth certificate.

Young Saul Feldstein was called to the telephone in his dormitory. He asked, "Who is it?"
The reply came, "It's your parents."
Saul said, "Hang up. I don't have parents."

The dorm adviser, a teacher, heard the reply, came over, and said, "What do you mean, you don't have parents?"

Saul said, "I go to boarding school in the winter, camp during the summer, and my grandparents' houses on vacation. I don't have parents, I have travel agents."

What ransom note did the rich Jewish parents receive?
"Give us one million dollars in small bills, or we guarantee you'll see your kid again."

How did the Jewish kid know his parents didn't like him?
When they went to the beach, the parents paid the lifeguard fifty dollars to keep his eyes off him.

What's Jewish blackmail?
You buy your daughter a new Mercedes, or she moves back in with you.

How did the Jewish mother know old age was coming?
It hit her from the rear.

How do Jewish kids celebrate their birthdays?
They send letters of congratulations to their parents.

Two Jewish couples went to Atlantic City for the weekend. While the men were shooting craps, the women wandered around the casino. They stopped to watch the roulette wheel spin. The little ball dropped into a slot, and a man who had wagered a hundred dollars on that number received a huge stack of chips worth four thousand dollars.

"That's so exciting," one woman said. She took out a hundred-dollar bill, then asked her friend, "What number should I play?"

The friend said, "Play your age."

The woman put the hundred-dollar bill on number "32." When the ball dropped into slot number "41," she fainted.

Why is a gynecologist like a Jewish mother?
They're both spreaders of old wives' tails.

Mrs. Teitlebaum picked up the telephone in her Miami Beach hotel suite and called room service.

"Your order, please," a voice said.

Mrs. Teitlebaum said, "I'd like two eggs scrambled until they're as dry as the sand on the beach. I'd like one bagel burned black with a speck of cream cheese so small you can hardly see it. And I'd like a pot of coffee that tastes like dishwater."

"Madam" the room-service person said, "we don't serve a breakfast like that."

"You did yesterday," she snapped.

The waiter approached the table where Morris Berkowitz was treating his mother to brunch. He said, "Was everything satisfactory, madam?"

She looked up and said, "I get more nourishment biting my lip."

What's a genius?
An average student with a Jewish mother.

Mrs. Feldstein took her son to the beach. The moment she sat down, she began barking at him.

"Joshua, don't get close to the water. You'll drown.

"Joshua, don't play in the sand. If it gets in your eyes, you'll go blind.

"Joshua, get out of the sun. You'll get skin cancer."

She paused for a moment, turned to the woman next to her, and said, "That Joshua of mine, he's such a nervous child."

What's the plural of yenta?
Hadassah.

Why do Jewish mothers give so much free advice?
That's all it's worth.

What do you call a Jewish boy with six sisters?
A whine connoisseur.

How do you know a Jewish kid is dumb?
His parents go to PTA meetings under an alias.

How do morticians make dead Jewish mothers look natural?
They leave their mouths open.

Little Myron had wandered away from his mother in the parking lot of the mall. Before she found him, he'd dashed between parked cars and was hit by a car. The boy lay on the ground with two broken legs, three cracked ribs, and a concussion. While waiting for the ambulance to arrive, his mother knelt and said, "Myron, I get you home and give you an enema, you'll be fine."

Myra met her friend Sophie at the butcher's. Sophie asked, "So how have you been?"

Myra sighed. "Don't ask. Three months ago, my Myron died of AIDS he caught from his secretary. Two months ago my daughter was in an auto accident and her legs were amputated. Then last week, my son left his wife and children to move to San Francisco with another man." Myra paused to wipe her eyes. "And that's not the worst."

"What else could be wrong?" Sophie asked.

"Tomorrow the painters are coming."

"My mother is the most fanatical housekeeper in the world," Mel Goldstein said to a friend.

"How so?"

"Last time I was home, I got up in the night to go to the bathroom. When I got back, my bed was made."

Sheldon Slotkin got a call at the office from his mother. "Tell me, Sheldon," she asked. "Saturday is your fortieth birthday. What special present do you want from your mother."

Sheldon replied, "You mean I can ask for anything?"

"Anything for my little boy."

"How about five minutes of silence," he said.

The Jewish husband was taking off his jacket in the front hall when his wife picked a telltale hair from his shoulder.

"Aha!" she exclaimed. "A gray hair. You've been sneaking off to your mother's again."

Little Julius was turning two, and his mother started to think about the celebration. She picked up the telephone book, turned to the city government listings, ran her fingers up and down the columns, found the number, and dialed.

The phone rang, then a voice answered, "Game warden."

"Oh, good," she said. "Tell me, what games do you recommend for two-year-olds."

How pessimistic are Jewish mother?
They read Horatio Alger novels backward.

Little Sydney walked into the house after school. His mother said, "So how did you do on that test, Sydney?"

He said, "I nearly got a hundred."

She beamed. "You mean, you got ninety-eight?"

"No," he replied. "Two zeros."

The teacher said to the class, "I want you to tell me who was the greatest man who ever lived. Whoever gives me the best answer gets a coupon for a free meal at McDonald's."

She called on an Italian kid, who replied, "Columbus."

"Good answer," she said. She pointed to an Irish girl, who replied, "St. Patrick."

"Fine," the teacher said. "Now, Leroy, what do you say?"

"Martin Luther King," the black boy said.

The teacher said, "That's the best answer of all. I'll give one more try to Irving."

The Jewish kid stood up and said, "The greatest man who ever lived was Jesus Christ."

The teacher beamed. "I'm pleased, Irving. You win the coupon."

After class, a friend came up to Irving and asked him about his answer. Irving replied, "Actually, I think Moses was the greatest man who ever lived. But business is business."

The teacher asked the little Jewish boy what the four seasons were.

The kid replied, "I only know two seasons—busy and slack."

Who is the Jewish husband's dream woman? His mother.

Where do you find a Jewish couple who have lived in perfect happiness for a decade?
Look for a Jewish mother and her ten-year-old son.

Why did the Jewish mother bring a broom to the wedding?
To bring the rice home for dinner.

What happened when the Jewish mother found her son jerking off in the bathroom?
She told him to stop or he'd go blind; he asked if he could keep going until he needed glasses.

How ugly was the Jewish kid?
His mother hung a lamb chop around his neck so the dog would play with him.

Why did the Jewish mother have her ashes scattered in Bloomingdale's?
So her daughter would visit her at least twice a week.

Did you hear about the new Jewish Mother Bank?
When you phone in, it whines, "You never visit. You never write. And you only call when you want money!"

What's a disadvantaged Jewish child?
One who drives a domestic automobile.

How can you tell a JAP mother?
She can hold a safety pin in her mouth and sip Perrier at the same time.

A Jewish man picked up the phone and dialed. When a voice answered, he asked, "Mother, how are you?"
"Fine."
"Sorry, I have the wrong number."

What's the difference between a Jewish mother and a vulture?
A vulture waits until you're dead to eat your heart out.

A friend walked into the hospital waiting room and saw Mrs. Schwartz sitting nervously in a seat. She walked up and asked, "How is your husband?"

Mrs. Schwartz shook her head. "Let me put it this way—if he were alive, he would be a very sick man."

What's the difference between a Jewish mother and an Italian mother?
An Italian mother says, "If you don't eat everything on your plate, I'll kill you." A Jewish mother says, "If you don't eat everything on your plate, I'll kill myself."

The Jewish boy came in from playing one day and asked, "Mother, why is it that blood rushes to my head when I turn upside down, but it doesn't rush to my feet when I stand up?"

His mother said, "Because your feet aren't empty."

What's a Jewish mother?
Someone who will forgive and forget, but who never forgets what she forgave.

The teacher announced that she was going to collect money for starving homeless children that day. She went around the room holding out a jar to each child. Annie put in a quarter, Billy put in a dime, Leroy contributed a nickel, and Sheldon dropped in a pledge.

What did the Jewish college girl do on her summer vacation?
Her hair and nails.

What's a Jewish dropout?
A boy who doesn't finish medical school.

CHAPTER 6

GREAT JOKES ABOUT JEWISH HOMOSEXUALS

Why is a lesbian like an Israeli lobbyist?
They both spend most of their time stroking
Bush.

Did you hear about the gay Jewish weight lifter?
He's always off in the corner, pumping Myron.

"Hey, Melvin," one gay called to his roommate,
"has the rabbi come yet?"
"No," Melvin panted, "but he's starting to
moan."

Why are so many homosexuals Jewish?
If you grew up with a Jewish mother, what
would you be?

Did you hear about the Jewish homosexual who
was eaten by an alligator?
He loved every minute of it.

A very swishy Jewish boy came along with his mother to visit their new neighbors, the Whitneys. While the mothers talked, the two boys went into the family room. But a few minutes later, the Whitney boy came running out of the room sobbing.

The Jewish mother went up to her son and said, "Bruce, what did you do?"

"Nothing, Mother darling. That sweet little thing just asked me to play Nintendo. So I put my hand on his goy stick."

Why are Jewish homosexuals lousy businessmen? They're all suckers.

Did you hear about the two Jewish gays who raped a girl?
One held her down while the other did her hair.

Why is a lesbian like a JAP?
They both love to eat out every night.

Why are Jewish gays such pricks?
You are what you eat.

Why aren't Jewish gays lonely?
They have friends up the ass.

The Waldensteins were thrilled when their only son fulfilled their dreams and went off to college. But they were very concerned two years later when the dean of students called them into his office. "I've got some good news and some bad new," the dean said.

Mr. Waldenstein said, "Give us the bad news."

"I'm afraid your son is a flamboyant homosexual," the dean said.

Mrs. Waldenstein nearly fainted. As she struggled to regain her composure, her husband said, "What could possibly be the good news?"

"Your son has been elected Homecoming Queen."

The Jewish gay walked into the doctor's office for a routine exam. He was lying on his stomach when the doctor discovered a string protruding from his butt. When the doctor pulled, a dozen roses came out.

"Hey," the doctor said, "do you know you've got a dozen roses stuck up your ass?"

"Really?" the gay replied. "Who are they from?"

Did you hear about the gay Old Testament?
The first couple was Adam and Steve.

Did you hear about the two Jewish gays who
had an argument at a cocktail party?
They went outside and exchanged blows.

Did you hear about the Jewish transvestite who
was arrested?
The charge was male fraud.

Did you hear about the Jewish interior decorator
who was all black and blue after an auto
accident?
He committed suicide because he clashed with
his drapes.

A very swishy Jewish man walked into a
florist and said, "Can you wire flowers home
to my mother?"
"Of course," the florist replied.
"Then send me to New York. I'm a pansy."

What do rabbis do with foreskins after circumcisions?
Sell them to gays for chewing gum.

How can you tell you're in a gay temple?
Half the congregation is kneeling.

How did the Jewish boy feel when he first discovered he was a homosexual?
It was quite a blow.

Why was the Jewish salesman at Bloomingdale's considered a pervert?
He went out with women.

What do you call a Jewish fairy?
A He-Blew.

Why do so many gay Jewish men have mustaches?
To hide the stretch marks.

How do so many Jewish men become homosexuals?
About 40 percent are born that way; the rest are sucked into it.

Why did the Jewish lesbian emigrate to Israel?
She missed the Hebrew tongue.

How do you get a Jewish fairy off your back?
Beat him off.

Did you hear about the Jewish boy who moved to San Francisco?
He turned prematurely gay.

How did the Jewish guy know he'd spent the night in a gay bar?
He woke up with a queer taste in his mouth.

Why do so few Jewish fairies play a musical instrument?
They always forget to blow instead of suck.

Why did the Jewish gay strip naked and tie a string around his dick before going to the costume party?
He was going as a pull toy.

CHAPTER 7

GREAT JOKES ABOUT OLDER JEWS

Two old Jewish ladies were sitting on a park bench complaining about their husbands. One said to the other, "Myron's losing his mind. Last week he went out and spent six hundred dollars on a water bed."

"A water bed?" the other lady repeated. "It sounds to me like he has some excitement in mind."

"I should die of excitement," the first lady replied. "The way he's been performing the last few years, that water bed could be called the Dead Sea!"

Two old ladies were sitting in the park when one said to the other, "Sadie, how is Saul treating you in bed these days."

Sadie replied, "He makes love just like a postman."

"What do you mean?"

Sadie grimaced. "It takes him about a week to deliver."

Mrs. Goldstein was tottering down the street carrying two shopping bags when a man came up behind her, stuck a gun in her back, and snarled, "Give me your money."

The little old Jewish lady turned around, then examined the strapping young man. She said, "Young man, you should be ashamed of yourself. A man your size should be robbing banks instead of little old ladies."

Moe Dobkin made his way to the doctor's office, went in for some tests, then waited for the results. Finally, the physician called him into his office and said, "Moe, we had a mix-up on your tests, but neither alternative is good. I'm afraid you either have AIDS or Alzheimer's disease."

"Ugh," Moe replied. "What do I do?"

The doctor replied, "I'm not totally sure. But I can tell you this—if you remember the way home, don't fuck your wife."

Young Mort Berger was sleeping in the double bed with his grandfather so that they could get up to go to temple in the morning. During the night, the old man sat up in bed and said, "Mort, get up. Run in and get your grandmother. Hurry."

The boy grimaced. "Grandpa, calm down. That's *my* dick you're holding."

Old Mr. Bernstein entered the examining room and told the doctor, "You have to help me. I need something that will help me get it up once in a while."

The doctor went into his office, returned with a needle full of a clear liquid, then gave the man a shot. "That will be a hundred dollars," he said. Bernstein made a fuss, but paid.

Two days later, Bernstein came into the doctor's office beaming. He cheerfully asked for another shot. The doctor obliged, and when he was finished, Bernstein handed him two hundred-dollar bills. The doctor protested, "But it's only a hundred dollars for the shot."

Bernstein replied, "The second hundred's from my wife."

Eighty-one-year-old Sol Braverman married his twenty-three-year-old secretary. On their wedding night, she waited in bed while he got into his nightshirt. Finally, he emerged, climbed into bed, and held up the five fingers on his right hand.

"My goodness," she cried. "You want to do it five times?"

"No," he replied. "I want you to pick a finger."

Why do Jewish women spend so much time in the beauty parlor?
It takes four hours just to get an estimate.

Mr. Weinstein walked into the doctor's office and said, "I've got to have a prescription for Sex-Lax."

The doctor said, "You mean Ex-Lax."

Weinstein shook his head. "I don't have trouble going. I have trouble coming."

Irving Shelstein was on his deathbed, so he called his attorney in to discuss his estate. Shelstein said, "I leave my business, my homes, my stocks, my cars, and all my other assets to my wife."

The attorney said, "There's no problem with that. I'll have the papers drawn up in an hour."

"Wait," the dying man said. "I have one more clause. To inherit all I own, my wife must remarry within six months of my death."

"That's a strange request," the attorney said. "Why would you insist on that?"

"Because," Shelstein replied, "I want someone to be sorry that I died."

Why did old Mr. Cohen decide to spend all his money on himself?
He wanted to turn his heirs gray.

How can you tell if a Jewish matron has had a face-lift?
The beauty marks on her cheeks are nipples.

The businessman settled in his airplane seat and took out the contract he had to review before he landed in the next city. An old Jewish woman sat next to him, and no sooner had she fastened her seat belt than she started moaning, "Oh, I'm so thirsty. Oh, I'm so thirsty."

The businessman tried to concentrate on his contract, but it was no use. He leaned over and said to the woman, "Madam, we're taxiing down the runway now. The stewardess will get you a drink when we're up in the air."

The Jewish woman ignored him, continuing to moan, "Oh, I'm so thirsty."

Finally, the businessman couldn't stand it anymore. Even though the plane was speeding down the runway, he got out of his seat, made his way back to the rest room, filled a cup with water, and gave it to the woman.

She drank it down, and the businessman picked up his contract. Immediately, the woman moaned, "Oh, was I thirsty! Oh, was I ever thirsty."

The two old Jewish men were sunning themselves on a park bench when one said, "I can't satisfy my wife anymore. I try, but nothing happens."

The other said, "I have no problem."

"Really?"

"Yes. Every night I walk into the bedroom, stand in front of my wife, take off my clothes, and ask, 'Are you satisfied?' Then she nods and goes to sleep."

The Census Bureau researcher came to the Jewish Home for the Aged. To get some idea of the task in front of him, he knocked at the first door and a seventy-nine-year-old Jewish grandmother answered. The researcher introduced himself, then asked, "Madam, what would you say the death rate is around here."

She replied, "Oh, about one per person."

The elderly Jewish grandmother was fixing her son-in-law with the evil eye. Finally, he couldn't take it anymore. He said, "Why are you staring at me like that?"

"Because," she replied. "I can't figure out how an idiot like you can be the father of the smartest grandchildren in the world."

Sol Schwartz, age eighty-eight, limped into the doctor's office and said, "Doctor, my right knee hurts all the time. I can barely walk."

The doctor sat him down and said, "Mr. Schwartz, I'm afraid you're going to have to learn to live with it. You have to understand that leg has been doing its work for nearly nine decades."

Schwartz replied indignantly, "So you mean my left leg is ten years younger?"

CHAPTER 8

GREAT JOKES ABOUT ISRAEL

Why don't Israeli soldiers wear bullet-proof vests?
Because if they don't work, they can't get their money back.

A man walked out of a house in Belfast, Northern Ireland, one night. He turned a corner, then found himself confronted by an armed, masked man pointing an automatic weapon. "Halt," the man said. "Are you Protestant or Catholic?"

Immediately, the man breathed a sigh of relief. "Neither," he replied. "I'm Jewish."

The gunman pressed the trigger, riddling the man with bullets. Then he removed his mask and said, "I must be the luckiest Arab in Ireland tonight."

How do they take a census in Israel?
They roll a quarter down the street.

The Israeli was walking over a bridge when an Arab in a car tried to run him over. To escape, the Jewish man dived into the water. Unfortunately, he couldn't swim. "Help me," he screamed at two Palestinians who were watching from the back. But they ignored him as he went down for the first time.

"Help me, and I'll make you rich," he yelled as he surfaced. But the two ignored him and he went down for the second time.

He surfaced again. With his last breath, he yelled, "Yasir Arafat fucks camels." The furious Palestinians dived into the water, pulled him out, and beat him to a pulp.

The Frenchman, the German, and the Israeli were sitting in the café drinking coffee and talking about how they lived.

The Frenchman said, "When I go to work, I drive my ten-thousand-dollar Renault. On weekends, I drive my thirty-thousand-dollar Peugeot, and when I travel abroad, I always drive a fifty-thousand-dollar Citröen."

"Bah," scoffed the German. "I drive my ten-thousand-dollar Volkswagen to work. But on weekends, I drive a fifty-thousand-dollar BMW, and when I go abroad, I drive a seventy-five-thousand-dollar Mercedes."

"Very impressive," the Israeli said. "As for me, I take the bus to work. I drive a used Ford around on the weekends. But when I go abroad, I drive a five-hundred-thousand-dollar armored tank."

How did Israel win the Six Days War?
The Israelis waited until the Arabs threw grenades, picked them up, pulled the pins, and threw them back.

Did you hear about the Israeli settler who made money with his outhouse?
He rented the basement to an Arab.

What's the difference between Israel and yogurt?
Yogurt has culture.

Why do so many Israeli men have Arab mistresses?
Arabs suck.

Why is there no prostitution in Israel?
Israeli women can't give it away.

What was the first Israeli settlement?
Three cents on the dollar.

Five years ago, an American journalist visited a new Israeli settlement on the West Bank. Every day, he watched the Jewish settlers arrogantly stride out of town to the fields on the main road, making the Palestinians in the area wait until they had passed.

This year, the journalist returned to see how Israeli–Arab relations had changed. And he was surprised to see that every morning, the Israeli settlers stepped aside to let the Palestinians walk down the road first. He went up to the Jewish mayor and said, "What brought about this big change? Did you decide to let the Arabs go first out of a sense of fair play?"

"No," the mayor said. "Land mines."

Why is there so little crime in Israel?
Crime doesn't pay.

Why did the Israeli government stop sex-education programs for Palestinians?
The camel died.

Why is a Palestinian hooker like an Israeli gunboat?
They're both full of Jewish seamen.

How many Israelis does it take to change a light bulb?
A hundred. One to screw it in and ninety-nine to invade Lebanon to find one.

What rights to Israeli soldiers read to Palestinians they arrest?
"You have the right to remain dead . . ."

One Israeli came up to another and said, "Hey, did you hear about the seven Palestinian leaders who were killed resisting arrest?"

"No," the second Israeli said. "When did that happen?"

"Tomorrow," the first replied.

Did you hear that a group of Palestinian terrorists held up the Bank of Israel?
They got away with fifty million dollars in pledges.

Two Israeli officers had finally persuaded a couple of Arab officers captured in the Six Days War to talk. One Israeli asked, "Where did you get your strategy?"

"From the Russians," an Arab replied.

"I thought so. What was the plan they taught you?"

The Arab said, "First, we retreat and draw the enemy into our territory. Then we wait for the heavy winter snows . . ."

An Arab-American journalist was sent to Israel to do a series of feature stories. He drove to a West Bank town, looked around, but was unable to spot anyone to interview. He finally located an Israeli settler, went up to him, and asked, "Say, where do Palestinians hang out around here?"

The settler pointed. "See that big limb on the tree over there?"

A lone Palestinian terrorist attempted to assassinate the mayor of Jerusalem. The Israeli government announced a nationwide manhunt. To help local authorities, the government released seven different pictures of the terrorist, each taken from a different angle.

That afternoon, the Israeli minister of justice received a telephone call from the mayor of a West Bank settlement. The mayor said, "I just want you to know that we captured six of those terrorists, and all of them were shot dead trying to escape. We're chasing the seventh now."

A bus crowded with Palestinian laborers careened over the side of a bridge in a remote portion of the West Bank. It was nearly six hours later when the Israeli army arrived. The commander located the head of a group of Israeli settlers, who had been the first on the scene. Pointing to a mound of dirt, the settler said, "We buried eighty-nine Arabs in the mass grave over there."

"You mean all of them were killed in the accident?"

"Well," the settler said, "some of them said they weren't. But you know how those Arabs lie."

Why do Israeli soldiers shoot every Palestinian they see?
Their motto is, "Let God sort them out."

How do you get a Palestinian out of a tree?
Cut the rope.

CHAPTER 9

GREAT JOKES ABOUT JEWS AND SEX

Two Jewish housewives were talking about a neighbor. "One thing you can say about Sophie," one said to the other, "is that she always keeps the dietary laws."

"I know," the second said. "After she screws the milkman, she always waits six hours before screwing the butcher."

What's a Jewish porno film?
Fifty-five minutes of begging, five minutes of sex, and one hour of guilt.

Did you hear about the Jewish guy who borrowed ten thousand dollars from the bank to divorce his wife?
The bank called it a "home improvement loan."

What's a Jewish "10"?
A girl with four limbs and six million dollars.

How does a Jewish hooker get her clothes?
Hole sale.

What's a Jewish ménage à trois?
Two headaches and a hard-on.

What's the leading sexually transmitted disease
among Jews?
Headaches.

A hooker came up to a man in the garment
district and said, "Want to have a party?"

The man replied, "Okay. As long as we do it
the Jewish way."

"I don't know that one," she said. "I've done
it the French way and the Greek way, but
never the Jewish way. If you show me, I'll do it
for free."

"That's the Jewish way," the man replied.

Why do Jewish men get circumcised?
Because Jewish women won't touch anything
that isn't 20 percent off.

One guy was talking to another guy at the temple. The talk turned to their home life. One guy said to another, "My wife Sophie has a mouth that won't stop. I'd give anything for one day's truce in our household."

The second guy said, "One day isn't anything. My wife and I didn't have a single argument for twenty-seven years."

"That's astounding," the first guy said. "But what happened after twenty-seven years?"

"We met."

What's a Jewish husband's definition of happiness? Finding out his secretary is pregnant—and her boyfriend's going to marry her.

After an endless courtship, Henry finally persuaded his JAP girlfriend to say yes to his proposal. They got to their honeymoon on their wedding night and slipped under the covers, with Henry tingling with anticipation. He was delighted when the JAP snuggled up to him and said, "Honey, now that we're married, can I do anything I like?"

He smiled, "Of course you can."

So she rolled over and went to sleep.

What's different about Jewish swingers?
When they go to a wife-swapping party, they have to bring the maid.

The Jewish business owner walked over to a new secretary one day and said, "You're beautiful, my dear. Where have you been all my life?"

She glanced at his wrinkles, then replied, "Teething."

One hooker said to the other, "How's business?"

"Awful," the other said. "All I could scrape up was a blowjob for a ninety-year-old Jewish guy."

"Gross," the first said.

"No, Saperstein."

What's the best way for a Jewish husband to get aroused?
Think hard.

The Jewish attorney met a gorgeous young secretary at a bar. They had a few drinks, necked passionately in a cab, entered his apartment, tore their clothes off, and climbed into bed. As he pumped away, the guy said, "Oh, baby, don't you feel the electricity between us."

"I did," she grumbled. "Until I discovered your short circuit."

Why is a Jewish couple's bedroom like a nudist colony?
They're both places where nothing goes on.

A Jewish businessman who fancied himself a stud picked up a woman in a bar, bought her a couple of drinks, took her back to his apartment, and made passionate love to her. But as the guy lit up a cigarette, the girl hopped out of bed and said, "Boy, are you a lousy lover!"

The guy replied indignantly, "I don't see how you can say that after only two minutes."

How do you know a Jewish guy is a loser?
The only woman he's been in is the Statue of Liberty.

Once upon a time, there was a poor young Jewish boy who went to the city to find his fortune. He got a lowly job in the garment district, then went to night school to improve himself. At school, he met the beautiful daughter of a wealthy Jewish banker. They were mutually attracted and spent several evenings drinking coffee and discussing their studies.

Finally, the girl invited the young man to bring his parents to her house to meet her parents. Instead of disguising his humble background, the young lover told the girl that his parents were uneducated, poor, but still honorable people who would be proud that their son was in love with a girl so far above his humble station. After he finished, the girl rose without a word, stormed out of the cafeteria, and never spoke to him again.

What is the moral of this story? A man who tells the truth never gets screwed.

Weinstein walked into a bar and said to his friend, "Sorry I'm late. My secretary was eating lunch at her desk and spilled a cup of chili in her lap."

"What did you do?"

Weinstein replied, "I chewed her out."

What's a Jewish gentleman?
A guy who'll screw the black maid on the bed when he's wife's out, but makes her ride in the backseat on the way home.

What's the only way a Jewish guy can date a "10"?
Take out three twos and a four.

The Jewish couple were sitting in the car after the movies. He leaned over, embraced her, then started to neck. They continued for a few minutes. Then she pulled away and said to him, "What are you thinking about?"

He grinned. "The same thing you are."

"Good," she said. "We still have an hour before the mall closes."

What's the new cheap Jewish birth-control method?
She puts a stone in his shoe to make him limp.

What do you know about a Jewish girl who's father owns a deli?
She's full of baloney.

Bernie sat down next to Sol at the coffee shop. They were chatting for a while when Bernie asked, "So, are you getting some on the side?"

Sol grimaced. "I haven't had any in so long I didn't know they'd moved it."

Why don't Jewish women wear chastity belts?
Because Jewish men love to eat locks.

Why are Jews such optimists?
They cut some off before they know how long it's going to grow.

Why didn't the ticket taker let the Jewish guy into the live sex show?
All he had was a stub.

The Jewish wife was in the gynecologist's office at the conclusion of her annual checkup. The doctor said, "Everything checks out perfectly. As a matter of fact, you have the cleanest vagina I've ever seen."

"I should," she replied, "I have a colored man come twice a week."

What's a Jewish ménage à trois?
Using both hands to masturbate.

Sol Feldstein was in the locker room of the country club listening as the assistant pro bragged of his many triumphs with the fair sex. Finally, he couldn't stand in any longer. He walked over to the pro and said, "I'll bet you a hundred dollars that I'm longer soft than you are hard."

The assistant pro smirked. "You've got a bet. How long are you soft?"

Feldstein said, "About three years," and pocketed the hundred.

What's a Jewish businessman's idea of oral sex?
Talking about himself.

The Jewish guy was on top, pumping away. Finally, the hooker said, "Hey, let's get on with it."

The Jewish guy said, "What's wrong?"

The hooker said, "If you can't get any harder, the Messiah will come before you do."

Why does a Jewish man give more expensive presents to his mistress than his wife? When he's hard, he's soft, but when he's soft, he's hard.

Why do Jewish men find sex is like bridge? The most important thing is a good hand.

The Jewish girl bragged to her boyfriend, "I had my breasts insured for one million dollars by Lloyds of London."

"Really," the guy said. "What did you do with the money?"

Two Jewish guys were sitting in a bar confessing their most embarrassing moments. One guy related a story about his mother coming in his room to find him masturbating.

"That's not so bad," the other guy said. "That happens to lots of kids."

"I got caught last night," the first guy explained.

The secretary came in late and disheveled the next morning. She confessed to her friend that she'd slept with Mr. Cohen, the owner of the garment business.

"How could you?" the friend exclaimed.

"I had to," the secretary said. "He took me to a motel and he told the desk clerk I was his wife."

By the year 2000, 2 out of 3 Americans could be illiterate.

It's true.

Today, 75 million adults...about one American in three, can't read adequately. And by the year 2000, U.S. News & World Report envisions an America with a literacy rate of only 30%.

Before that America comes to be, you can stop it...by joining the fight against illiteracy today.

Call the Coalition for Literacy at toll-free **1-800-228-8813** and volunteer.

Volunteer Against Illiteracy. The only degree you need is a degree of caring.